THE HOW AND WHY WONDER BOOK OF
REPTILES
AND AMPHIBIANS

By ROBERT MATHEWSON, Curator of Science,
Staten Island Institute of Arts and Sciences, Staten Island, N.Y.
Illustrated by DOUGLAS ALLEN and DARRELL SWEET
Editorial Production: DONALD D. WOLF

Edited under the supervision of
   Dr. Paul E. Blackwood, Washington, D.C.

Text and illustrations approved by
   Oakes A. White, Brooklyn Children's Museum, Brooklyn, New York

GROSSET & DUNLAP • **Publishers** • **NEW YORK**

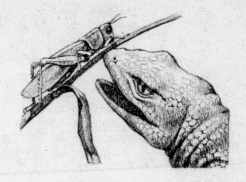

Introduction

There are five large groups of backboned animals on earth today. They are the amphibians, birds, fishes, reptiles and mammals. This *How and Why Wonder Book* deals with two of these groups — amphibians and reptiles.

Which snakes are poisonous and which ones are not? This seems to be an endlessly interesting question to most people. Equally interesting are the fantastic superstitions and misbeliefs about snakes. This book deals with both of these topics. It tells which snakes are poisonous and which ones are not. It tells about many of the common superstitions and provides correct information about them. In addition, it tells many other interesting things about amphibians and reptiles, such as their eating habits, how they protect themselves and how they move.

In the Space Age there is no lesser need for people with knowledge about all plant and animal life. This interesting and informative book on reptiles and amphibians may stimulate a potential young scientist to select *herpetology* (the study of reptiles) as his major field of interest.

Youthful herpetologists who wish to learn about the habits of reptiles by close observation will be glad to know that several of the reptiles make good pets. This *How and Why Wonder Book* tells which ones may easily be kept as pets and gives suggestions for collecting and keeping them.

Paul E. Blackwood

Dr. Blackwood is a professional employee in the U. S. Office of Education. This book was edited by him in his private capacity and no official support or endorsement by the Office of Education is intended or should be inferred.

Library of Congress Catalog Card Number: 72-86054

ISBN: 0-448-05008-0 (Wonder Book Edition)
ISBN: 0-448-04009-3 (Deluxe Edition)

1974 PRINTING

CONTENTS

VARANOSAURUS

EDAPHOSAURUS

Douglas Allen

The Age of Reptiles

In the beginning, warm seas flooded over much of the land, and there was life only in the water. During certain times of the year, the pools and lakes in which these sea creatures lived dried up, and many of the animals perished. But after millions of years, some of these creatures developed the ability to breathe dry air, and they became able to spend part of their lives on the land. These creatures were called amphibians, a name which comes from the Greek word meaning "two lives."

Many amphibians eventually began to spend more of their lives on land, and in time, they became better adapted to it. Finally, some of these creatures became able to live on the land all of the time, and these land-living animals were called reptiles, which comes from a Latin word meaning "crawler."

During the early Mesozoic period in the history of the earth, about 200 million years ago, the reptiles became the most important group of animals. Other reptile forms developed, including giant

DIMETRODONS

dinosaurs which roamed the land, great sea reptiles and dragon-like creatures which flew. The dinosaurs became so large and powerful that they ruled the world for more than 100 million years.

But the earth was changing. The climate, which had been warm, became cool. The swampy lands grew dry. The plant life on which dinosaurs had fed began to disappear. They were cold-blooded creatures and couldn't stand the cooler temperatures, and their huge size usually prevented them from seeking shelter in smaller caves. Plant-eating dinosaurs either couldn't find enough to eat or were unable to eat the newer kinds of plants. And when the plant-eaters died, the meat-eating dinosaurs were left without a source of food. The giant dinosaurs were not able to change, or adapt, with the changing world and eventually, they died out.

Although the giant reptiles died out, smaller forms did not and their relatives survive to this day. Why they survived is not certain. Perhaps the smaller reptiles were able to adapt to the changing conditions in the world.

Today, the living reptiles include the snakes, lizards, turtles, crocodilians (alligators, crocodiles and their relatives) and the tuatara.

Getting to Know the Reptiles

SCALY SKIN

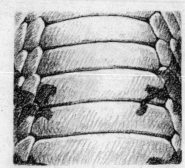

PLATED SKIN

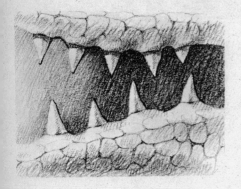

REPTILE TEETH

Scientists who have studied snakes and

Do snakes attack people?

their habits agree that snakes will avoid human beings whenever possible. Even the largest, most poisonous snakes strike only in search of food, or in fear of attack. To a snake, man is neither a natural enemy nor a source of food, and a snake only attacks a human being when it either does not sense his presence in time to slither away, or feels that its nest is endangered. All hikers should make it a practice to wear high boots in snake country, since the ankle and calf are the areas most vulnerable to snakebite.

The forked tongue which gives the snake its dangerous appearance is a harmless organ; it has nothing to do with the injection of venom. Since snakes have poor eyesight, they must constantly flick their tongue in order to smell what they cannot see. The base of the snake's tongue is connected to a smelling organ in the roof of its mouth. Thus the snake follows the trail of its prey by picking up the scent with its tongue.

COPPERHEAD HATCHING

Reptiles are vertebrates (backboned animals) which live in warm climates. They are cold-blooded and the temperature of their bodies is about the same as the temperature about them. Their skin is either smooth or scaly, or covered with shells or plates. Reptiles have lungs and breathe air. Their teeth are usually uniform in shape and size. They lay eggs or bear living young which look just like the adult reptiles.

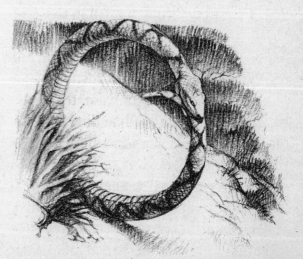

Snakes do not grasp their tails and roll downhill.

Snakes do not milk cows, goats or any other animal.

Young animals fear snakes only when taught to fear.

Snake venom is actually a kind of saliva that helps the snake digest its food. Venoms are complicated chemical substances that work in two ways: Some damage blood cells, causing uncontrollable bleeding; others kill by attacking the nerves so that heartbeat and breathing stop.

What is snake venom?

The poisonous venom is injected as the snake bites and sinks its long, curved, hollow fangs into its victim. Normally, these venom teeth are folded back, flat against the roof of the snake's mouth.

How is snake venom used in medicine?

The venoms of certain snakes are very useful in treating certain medical conditions. Rattlesnake venom is helpful in treating people who suffer from epileptic seizures. The venoms of water moccasins, vipers, and tiger snakes contain a substance that helps blood to clot, and are therefore helpful in controlling bleeding. Cobra venom is a powerful pain-killer. It helps control deep-seated pain more effectively than morphine, one of the most effective pain-killing drugs, but unlike morphine, cobra venom is not habit-forming.

How are snakes "milked"?

Collecting snake venom is a tricky and dangerous job. Despite leather gloves, people who do this work get bitten, and some have even died. The venom of a rattlesnake can be removed by prying open its mouth and pressing the venom gland in each cheek, which forces out the poison through the snake's hollow fangs. Since this procedure can be harmful to the snake, a better way is to let the snake bite through a rubber membrane stretched over the top of a collecting glass. This allows the angry snake to release its venom in a more natural way.

After the venom is collected, it is dried into crystals and tested for potency. The strength of the venom is measured in "mouse units" — the amount required to kill a mouse within a day. Cobra venom of fifty mouse units' strength (1/60,000 of an ounce) is used for control of pain in human beings. Snakes used for venom production must be force-fed through a tube, because a snake refuses to eat if it is handled too frequently.

The venom collected from various species of snakes can be used to prepare an antidote for the poison. This preparation, called an *antivenin*, contains diluted venom and is injected into a person who has been bitten by a poisonous snake.

WESTERN PAINTED TURTLE

D.A.

WOOD TURTLE

BOX TURTLE

GOPHER TORTOISE

YOUNG ELEGANT SLIDER

SPOTTED TURTLE

LEATHERBACK TURTLE (AQUATIC)

MUD TURTLE

LOGGERHEAD TURTLE

GREEN TURTLE

SNAPPING TURTLE

Are They Poisonous or Harmless?

The fact that some snakes are poisonous

Are all snakes poisonous?

is probably one of the main reasons why people fear them. Actually most reptiles are harmless. Of the 2,450 species of snakes in the world, only 175 kinds are dangerously poisonous.

A similar situation exists with the lizards. There are only two species which are poisonous: the Mexican beaded lizard and its first cousin, the Gila monster, or Gila, of Mexico and the United States. All the hundreds of other kinds of lizards that inhabit the world are nonpoisonous. There are no poisonous turtles or crocodilians (reptiles related to, and including, the crocodiles).

Another type of reptile which is non-poisonous is the tuatara, a lizard-like animal which occurs only in New Zealand. Some scientists consider the tu-

The Gila gets its name from the Gila River, Arizona.

The tuatara lives on coastal islands of New Zealand.

atara a living "fossil," because it is believed to have persisted in somewhat its present form for many millions of years.

It would be very convenient if all of the

Can you tell a poisonous snake from a harmless one?

poisonous snakes carried a "badge," or marking or shape, by which we could easily tell them from the harmless ones. All rattlesnakes are poisonous, and can be identified by a horn-like, loosely jointed rattle at the end of the tail. However, even this can be broken off accidentally.

But there is no single way by which we can tell whether an unknown snake is poisonous or harmless, unless, of course, we are willing to look into its mouth to see if it has fangs.

Some people say that if you smell

Can you locate poisonous snakes by their odor?

a cucumber odor while walking in the woodland a poisonous copperhead is nearby. To prove that this method of identifying snakes is risky, just ask your friends what a cucumber smells like. You will undoubtedly be given many different answers, which proves, of course, that you cannot locate copperheads or, for that matter, any snake, by their odor.

This is the safe and correct way of holding a snake.

Snake skulls: poisonous (left); nonpoisonous (right).

Another misleading belief about snakes is that if one has a **Can you tell a poisonous snake by the shape of its head?** triangular or diamond-shaped head it is poisonous. Some of the world's most dangerous snakes, including the king cobra of Malay, the black mamba of Africa and the coral snake of the United States, have blunt rounded heads. On the other hand, many of the water snakes in the United States and other countries have distinct triangle-shaped heads and are harmless. You cannot identify a poisonous snake simply by the shape of its head.

Another belief is that snakes with eyes **Can you tell a poisonous snake by the shape of its eyes?** that have round pupils are harmless, and those with elliptical pupils — like those of a cat — are poisonous. The cobras of India, Malay and Africa are all very poisonous and have eyes with round pupils, whereas the harmless night snake of the southwestern United States has elliptical pupils. So you cannot tell a poisonous snake merely by the shape of its eyes.

AFRICAN COBRA

BEADED LIZARD

CHUCKWALLA

WESTERN COLLARED LIZARD

DESERT SPINY LIZARD

GILA MONSTER

HORNED TOADS

One of the most popular errors about snakes is that all green-colored snakes are venomous. The green mamba of Africa is one of the most deadly snakes known, but the green snake from the northeastern United States is completely harmless; in fact, it will not even offer to bite. So all snakes that are green in color are not necessarily poisonous.

Are green-colored snakes poisonous?

Not all snakes have the same kind of poison. Some have a somewhat similar poison, called a haemotoxin, a kind that affects the blood. These include the rattlesnakes, copperheads and moccasins of the United States and Mexico, as well as many of the vipers, such as Wagler's and temple vipers of Malay and Russell's and Gaboon vipers of Africa.

Do all snakes have the same kind of poison?

Cobras of Africa, Malay and India, tiger snakes of Australia, and coral snakes of the southeastern United States, as well as many others, have neurotoxins, a poison which affects the nerves. Some amount of each type of poison is present in the venom of each kind of snake, so if we are to be treated for snakebite we shall have to use the serum for the particular snake that did the biting.

No animals have been the victims of more fanciful tales than have the reptiles. In fact, some of the stories are quite silly — stories such as: "There are snakes that can take their tails into their mouths and roll downhill like a hoop"; "Turtles live for a million years"; "If a snake's head is cut off, the snake will continue to live until sundown"; "There are snakes that will wrap around your legs and whip you with their tails"; "There are snakes which can milk a cow"; "Alligators, like turtles, can live almost forever." These statements are all false, of course.

Are all stories about reptiles true?

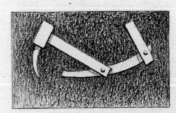

Two tubes lead from the snake's poison glands or sacs to its fangs, which are hollow. When the snake bites its victim, poison from the glands is squeezed through the fangs. The illustrations (right to left) show a rattlesnake head, skull, mechanical action of the jaws, and poison sac location (dark area). Only when injected is venom poisonous.

The twelve-foot-long boa constrictors of tropical America prey on birds and mammals.

A unique poisonous snake is the African spitting cobra. This reptile, about three to four feet in length, lives in the jungle. It not only injects its poison by biting, but when its prey or an enemy approaches, it raises its forward end off the ground and by quickly flicking the head forward, ejects small droplets of venom from the tips of its hollow fangs. At the same instant it exhales with a sharp hiss. The poison thus sprayed gets into the eyes of the victim and causes considerable harm, particularly if the eyes are rubbed.

Can snakes spit their poison?

The poisonous Gila monster and the Mexican beaded lizard do not have hollow teeth. Their venom glands are situated in the lower jaws. They cannot poison their prey unless they chew and get the venom into the victim.

How do lizards inject poison?

What Do They Eat?

The nonpoisonous snakes use other methods to catch their prey. Many are constrictors that grasp the food with their teeth and then throw loops of their bodies, in coils, around the victim. Usually, they kill not by crushing the animal, but by preventing it from breathing. Both big snakes and little snakes use this constricting method to kill their prey.

How do the nonpoisonous snakes capture their prey?

Some of the big snakes which do this are the regal python of Malay, which reaches a length of thirty feet; the twelve-foot boas and twenty-five-foot anacondas of South America; and the fifteen-foot pythons from India. Smaller ones are the mountain blacksnake from the northeastern United States and the California king snake, as well as hundreds of others.

The nonconstrictors catch their food by either grasping

How do the nonconstrictors catch food?

with the mouth and pressing the prey beneath their body or by merely swallowing it whole. All snakes swallow their food whole, because they do not have chewing or grinding teeth. Their teeth are shaped like curved needles, which hook into the prey, holding and manipulating it into the snake's throat. Their jaws are loosely connected at the skull and chin and this peculiar arrangement enables them to open their mouths very wide. Further, their overlapping body scales can be spread apart, so that bulky food can be swallowed.

A twenty-five-foot regal python can easily devour a half-

Do they eat large animals?

grown pig. A meal of this size usually takes more than an hour to swallow. Then the snake finds a suitable hiding place and may stay there more than two weeks before the meal is completely digested. The snake extends its windpipe out of the side of its mouth, like a snorkle, enabling it to breathe while eating the pig.

Lizards, turtles and crocodilians also have interesting

How do lizards catch food?

feeding habits. The African chameleon lizard captures food with its tongue. These six-to-eight-inch lizards slowly move through the bushes and trees, clasping small limbs with their clawlike feet, while their eyes are constantly searching for insects. The eyes protrude at each side of the head and each eye can look in a different direction at the same time.

When an insect is discovered, the lizard slowly approaches until it is about its own body length away. Suddenly, with tremendous speed, the tongue shoots out and the insect disappears down the lizard's throat. The tongue is almost as long as the lizard and is tipped with a sticky, fleshy end which adheres to the prey. Almost before the insect can move, it finds itself drawn into the lizard's mouth. African chameleons have the ability to change color and usually match their surroundings so well that they are hard to find.

The American chameleon of the southeastern United States and islands of the Caribbean, while not true chameleons, can also change their body colors. These are the small lizards which are sold at the circus or pet shop. They can run very fast, and they capture insects by pouncing upon them.

How Do They Move?

Turtles move slowly as they walk, but there are times when

Can turtles move fast?

they can move very fast. The surprisingly quick lunges of the eighteen-inch common snapping turtle of the eastern United States and the large alligator snapping turtle of the Mississippi River can be dangerous, especially if we get too close to their strong jaws.

The mata mata turtle of Guiana and northern Brazil, when feeding, moves so fast that we can hardly follow the motion.

American alligator

Heads of alligator (left) and crocodile (right). The alligator's snout is broad and rounded while the crocodile's is pointed and its head is narrower.

What are the crocodilians?

The crocodilians are a species of reptile descended from a giant fifty-foot crocodile that lived a hundred million years ago during the age of dinosaurs. The 23-foot-long Orinoco crocodile, in Venezuela, is the largest crocodile living today. In the United States, there are two crocodilians, the American crocodile and the American alligator.

Both of these creatures are covered with heavy scales and are amphibious, but the crocodile is a salt-water creature, found only in the southernmost part of Florida, while the alligator lives in the fresh-water swamps of Florida, Georgia, and Louisiana. Both crocodiles and alligators vary in length from about ten to fourteen feet.

These fearsome reptiles are heavily armored with scales, and a ridge of bony plates extends along their spine. You can distinguish an alligator from a crocodile by looking at its head. An alligator has a more rounded snout and all its teeth are hidden when its mouth is shut. A crocodile has a longer, more pointed mouth, with a large tooth exposed on each side when its mouth is closed.

These reptiles swim with a snakelike motion, with the help of their webbed feet, and can kill their prey with a single blow of their powerful tail. Their jaws clamp down with crushing force, and once closed, cannot be forced open. But a man can close the jaws and hold them shut, a dangerous feat practiced by alligator "wrestlers." So-called "crocodile tears" are actually salty secretions from glands in the animal's head.

The American crocodile lays its eggs in a hole it digs in the sand; the American alligator builds a mound of twigs and leaves, deposits its eggs on top, and covers them up. Crocodiles can live to be fifty years old. They do not normally attack human beings. Alligators have excellent hearing, and a powerful, bellowing voice that they rarely use.

of the world including Africa, Mexico, Central and South America, and the southern United States. Alligator hunters say that some of these reptiles can move, for short distances, faster than a man can run.

No movement of any animal, even the lithe gait of the tiger **How do snakes move?** or the wavy movements of the caterpillar, is more graceful than the slithering flow of the snake. Armless and legless, they move across the surface of

forward part of the body is stretched out until it touches another rough spot, such as a rock. If this spot is held with a crook of the body, the tail can then be drawn up and placed at this spot, too, and in this way, the snake's body can be pushed or pulled forward.

There are many rough spots that a snake can use and if it inches its body over all the rough spots, it then moves smoothly along the ground or appears to flow up trees. If you place a small snake upon a smooth piece of glass, its movement is similar to that of a cater-

FLYING LIZARD

the ground or climb trees with great ease. If we watch carefully we can soon understand how they move.

First the tail is held against a rough spot, such as a clump of grass. Then the

pillar. These two main types of locomotion are used by most snakes.

The sidewinder rattlesnake of the southwestern United States **How do desert snakes move?** and the desert viper of Africa live on the soft shifting sands of the desert and, for this reason, crawl with another kind of motion. By throwing loops of its body forward, the desert snake can lift the remaining part of its body off the sand, bringing it up to the forward loop. This causes it to move with a sidewinding motion, and is the reason for the name "sidewinder."

The most unusual kind of travel practiced by snakes is used **Can any snakes fly?** by the flying snakes of Malay. These colorful reptiles, fifteen to eighteen inches in length, are arboreal (tree-dwellers),

escape by running across the surface of the water. The toes of these lizards are provided with flaps, which are erected as the lizards run. This causes the foot to become a flat pad, which provides a surface sufficient to support their weight on top of the water. When they are far enough away from danger, they stop running and sink out of sight.

Some small desert lizards, such as the sand skink, escape their enemies by diving into loose sand. Then, by a swimming motion, they progress quite rapidly beneath the surface. The geckos, a

GECKO

Flying lizards glide from tree to tree with the aid of their folds of skin. The harmless, ridge-toed gecko gets its name from the cry it makes.

and when they choose to go from place to place, particularly in times of danger, they flatten out the body and slide off into space. The great width of the flattened body enables them to glide to the ground or to another limb, and in this way they escape.

The basiliscus lizards, eight to twelve inches long, live along the **How do lizards move?** edges of swamps and rivers in Central America. When chased by an enemy, they

group of small lizards living in the warm countries the world over, have ridges across their toes which act somewhat like suction devices. This enables them to run across a smooth surface, and they are often seen running along the ceilings of houses in pursuit of insects.

The sea turtles are very ancient types of reptiles that have existed in somewhat their present form for more than 150 million years. Graceful swimming movements with flipper-like legs give them the appearance of flying through the water.

Are Reptiles Valuable?

Where do sea turtles lay their eggs? These large marine reptiles stay in the ocean throughout most of their lives, coming ashore only to lay their eggs. In the evening, in early summer, many of the females come from the waters of the tropical Atlantic and Pacific to visit the sandy beaches along the coasts of the United States, Mexico, Central and South America. They make their way to a place above the high-tide mark, where they scoop out a shallow basin in the sand. In a period of two to three hours a turtle will lay from 100 to 150 eggs in this "nest." She then spends some time covering the clutch (a nest of eggs) by pushing and patting sand into it. No further care is given the eggs and they are left to the warm moist sand until they hatch. Turtles do not sit on their eggs as birds do.

Can we eat the eggs of sea turtles? Fishermen along these beaches will seek out such nests, for the eggs are good to eat. The adult turtles are also sought as food. A prize catch is the large Atlantic green sea turtle, which weighs between 150 and 200 pounds. Its meat is tasty and it is also used for making turtle soup.

In what ways are reptiles valuable to us? Before the advent of plastics, the shells of hawksbill sea turtles, which measure from twenty to thirty inches, were extensively used for making fancy buttons and rims for eyeglasses.

The turtles (above) are laying eggs and covering them with sand for both warmth and protection. At the right is a snapping turtle hatching from its egg.

In many shops we find leather goods made from the hides of alligators, snakes and lizards, including such items as purses, wallets, handbags, shoes, belts and many other articles. Not too long ago the Florida State Conservation Department had to pass a law forbidding people to take alligators from that state, lest they become extinct. Most of the leather now used to make these articles is imported from South America.

At Silver Springs, Florida and at San Butanton, Brazil, there are large snake farms where venom is extracted from poisonous snakes. This venom is processed and used as a medicine, which is very effective in treating certain kinds

part of their diet is made up of insects and rodents. It has been estimated that rodents destroy foodstuffs worth over 200 million dollars each year, so anything that preys on rats, mice, gophers and similar vermin is a good and valuable friend of man.

Reptiles of many kinds are found in the temperate and tropical countries of the world. They are of many different shapes, sizes and colors. One example is the thirty-foot giant gavial of Africa, a crocodile-like animal which lives along the Nile River and has an extremely long snout. Another is the wormlike blind snake, eight to twelve inches long, that lives beneath the ground in the southwestern United States and in Mexico. There are many forms that are only rarely seen, and others are commonly found near our homes.

How can we get to know more about reptiles?

of human sickness. Snake venom is also used to make the serum for the treatment of snake bite.

A small industry has been started in Florida for the canning of rattlesnake meat for food.

Perhaps the greatest service reptiles render to man arises from the fact that reptiles like to eat, and that the larger

A great deal of fun and education can be had by reading about the many kinds and by visiting zoos and museums where living specimens can be studied. However, the most interesting way to learn more about these animals is to go afield and collect them. The following lizards, turtles and snakes are not only interesting, but they are easily collected.

The lizard's tail, torn off by a bird, will regenerate (grow back to original form).

21

Turtles

PAINTED TURTLE

Spotted Turtle

The round orange-yellow spots on the black carapace (top shell) give the spotted turtle its name. These turtles, three to five inches long, are found throughout the eastern United States, where they live in the quiet waters of small ponds, lakes or swamps. Occasionally, they migrate from one pond to another and at these times they seek out the damp places on the woodland floor. Like many of the aquatic turtles, spotted turtles feed only when they are in the water. They use water to wet the food, thereby making a meal easier to swallow. Their food consists of worms, insects, fish and some aquatic plants.

How did the spotted turtle get its name?

The common spotted turtle makes a good house pet.

Specimens are found occasionally without spots and these can be identified by the smooth shell and the orange-yellow bands on the head. They make excellent pets, which soon become tame and feed from the hand.

Painted Turtle

This is one of the more common pond turtles that are often seen sunning themselves on a rock or floating log in the middle of a pond. When disturbed, they quickly slide into the water and bury themselves in the soft bottom mud or debris. They are easily identified by the mottled yellow to orange-red border of both the carapace and plastron (bottom shell). These markings and the stripes of yellow, red and black on the head are reasons for the name "painted turtle."

How did the painted turtle get its name?

They are found throughout the United States, except in the extreme west. They rarely leave the water where they catch their food—insects, salamanders, worms and fish. Young specimens are very attractive and are often sold by animal dealers and in pet shops.

BOX TURTLE

deep rich brown. A specimen which had been in captivity for some five years became so tame, that whenever it was hungry, it would patiently wait near a feeding dish for its dinner.

Gopher Tortoise

The names tortoise, terrapin and turtle are really interchangeable. However, the word "tortoise" is generally used to name the kind that live in arid places, such as the Galapagos Islands off the coast of Ecuador. These islands are the home of the giant Galapagos tortoises that grow three feet in length. The names turtle and terrapin are usually used to describe those that live in or near the water.

Should we say "tortoise" or "terrapin" or "turtle"?

The gopher tortoises found in the United States live in sandy regions in many of the southern states between South Carolina and Texas. Unlike the other turtles, whose feet are flat and

The burrows of the gopher tortoise give it its name.

Box Turtles

Because of a broad hinge across the forward third of the plastron, box turtles can draw up their lower shell inside of the carapace. In this way they can completely "box" in all of the soft parts of their bodies as a protection against enemies.

How does a box turtle protect itself?

These turtles are favored as pets. They have a friendly disposition and can be freely handled. They are often seen roaming through woodlands and fields, particularly after a heavy rain, seeking insects, worms, berries and green vegetation. They are not aquatic, but they do not hesitate to enter the water and sometimes are found bathing.

There are four kinds in the United States, found from Texas to the Atlantic coast. All have yellow to yellow-orange stripes or markings on a carapace of webbed and adapted for swimming, the tortoises have stumpy feet which are better suited for travel over the dry ground. The gopher tortoises make their homes in tunnels which they dig in the loose earth. At the far end of the tunnel, they excavate a small "room" in which they can turn about. In the wild they feed upon berries, grasses and insects. Specimens taken as pets can be fed berries, lettuce, apples and other fruit. In captivity, these reptiles like a pan of water in which they soak for long periods of time. Perhaps in the wild they get a great deal of moisture in their burrows.

The diamondback eats plants, worms and shellfish.

Diamondback Turtle

These turtles can be found along the Atlantic coast from Maine to Florida, and in the Gulf of Mexico from Florida to Texas. They live in salt and brackish water marshes and bays. At one time they were heavily hunted for food, but now their numbers are increasing. Small specimens are particularly attractive. However, collectors will find it difficult to keep them alive unless the turtles are provided with a tank of marine water with ample circulation. Adults can either be caught in the marshes or purchased at local fish markets.

The plastron is yellowish in color and **How did it get its name?** the large scales on the carapace have a series of whitish grooves, outlined against a gray-black color. The grooves, which are more or less diamond-shape in outline, are the reason for the name "diamondback." Many turtle farms where these specimens are raised are situated along the coast between Maryland and Florida.

Pacific Turtle

The good nature of the Pacific turtle makes it an excellent pet. **Can you feed it by hand?** It is very responsive when taken into captivity, and soon loses its fright. It will take food from the hand and, if regularly fed at a certain time, it will always be found waiting. It is a relative of the eastern spotted turtle, but is found only in the lakes, ponds and quiet streams along the Pacific Coast between Washington and California. Faint traces of yellow are found on the carapace, which has a ground color of soft olive-brown, and there is a mottling of yellow along the sides of the plastron. This reptile feeds upon crayfish, insects, some plants and fresh fish.

Giant green sea turtles are found in large numbers on the Atlantic beaches of North and South America. In Florida and other places, they have been hunted down to near-extinction because they make excellent turtle soup. These clumsy 350-pound reptiles intrigue naturalists, who have discovered that the turtles swim thousands of miles every year across the Caribbean Sea and the South Atlantic.

Why do green turtles migrate?

To track their migrations, Dr. Archie Carr, a zoologist, has used balloons attached by a line to the turtles' shells. The balloons float in the air even while the turtles swim underwater. He has also clipped metal tags to the flippers of thousands of turtles nesting on the beaches of Central America. Later, he found tagged turtles scattered among Caribbean islands as far as 1,500 miles away.

Dr. Carr concluded that the turtles' *nesting grounds,* where they mate and lay their eggs, are far removed from their *pasture grounds,* where they live and feed most of the time. Every two or three years, the green sea turtle leaves its pasture grounds and swims a long, slow course to its island nesting place. Once there, the females scramble up the beach, and dig shallow holes in the sand with their flippers. There they later deposit their eggs.

One of the most famous nesting grounds for green turtles is Ascension Island, a small isolated rock in the middle of the South Atlantic. The turtles do not live there, but return to the island every two or three years. To discover the extent of their wanderings, Dr. Carr

The migrations of sea turtles are tracked with the help of balloons attached to their shell.

tagged the Ascension Island turtles. He later found the tagged specimens on the beaches of Brazil, 1,400 miles away.

Dr. Carr wondered how a green turtle, swimming across the open ocean, could unerringly find its way to this rocky nesting ground, a mere dot on the map of the South Atlantic. He deduced that the turtle may use the stars, sun, or moon to guide it to the general area of Ascension Island. Once near the island, it recognizes the odor of the place where it was born, and follows the scent directly to its nesting ground.

How does the green turtle navigate?

Lizards

It is easy to recognize the resemblance between the present-day lizards and the giant dinosaurs. Many millions of years ago, during the period when dinosaurs roamed the earth, there were many smaller reptiles clambering among the rocks at the feet of these giants. These smaller reptiles, which were the ancestors of our modern lizards, could easily hide from the "giants" and probably, in many instances, raided their nests and ate their eggs. It is possible that the smaller size of these early lizards, and their lesser need for food, helped them to survive, while the giant dinosaurs died out.

Why did the ancestors of the lizards survive?

The Black Komodo Dragon, also called the Komodo monitor, is the world's largest lizard. It lives on the island of Komodo and on a few other small, rocky islands off the coast of Java, Indonesia. These ten-foot-long carnivores eat monkeys, wild boars, and even small deer, which they swallow whole, as snakes do. Like snakes, they have a long forked tongue that they use to smell out decaying animals.

What is the largest lizard?

KOMODO DRAGON

The bearded lizard wears its "collar." When it is frightened, it extends the frills of skin around its neck.

One blow of their powerful tail is usually sufficient to kill their prey. After a meal, they become sluggish and may sleep and fast for days. The younger Komodo monitors catch rats, snakes, and fish. They occasionally climb trees to raid birds' nests, and even dig up and eat their own eggs. About two thousand Komodo monitors now live on the "dragon islands," along with a few hundred people. Although the Komodo monitor's ancestors may have swum long distances to reach the islands thousands of years ago, today these giant lizards rarely swim far from their home.

Glass Snake

This long, slender, legless reptile looks like a snake. However,

How does the glass snake trick enemies?

it has both eyelids and ear openings, which are never found in snakes. Glass snakes can be found in the

southeastern and central parts of the United States. Like many other lizards, they can break off their tails while being captured. This act is often a good defense, because the broken tail does not hurt the lizard and, as the tail lies wrig-

GLASS SNAKE

gling on the ground, it attracts the attention of the enemy. Meanwhile, the intact body of the lizard — minus the tail — crawls away to safety.

The snakelike appearance of these lizards and their extremely long tails are

27

probably responsible for the false stories about "disjointed snakes that will survive." In captivity, these lizards feed readily on insects, worms and small lizards. If care is taken when they are caught, the tail and body may remain in one piece. Broken tails cannot rejoin the body, but the glass snake will grow a new short tail.

their hind legs. The forelegs are folded under the body at this time. With a little imagination, we can picture from this pose what some of the giant reptiles must have looked like millions of years ago.

Collared lizards make their homes in rocky arid places in the southwestern United States. They feed mainly upon

The long-tailed, thin-necked collared lizards are numerous in rocky areas of the southwestern United States.

Collared Lizard

If taken into captivity, these lizards soon refuse food and die. It is

How does it get its name? far wiser to study this lizard, which is ten to fifteen inch long, in the field.

Their name comes from the black or deep brown collar that girdles the neck. They are attractive but very nervous, and will usually bite if handled. If alarmed, they will race away on all four feet, lift the tail and forward part of the body off the ground, and run swiftly on

insects, but will also catch and eat small lizards.

Fence Lizards

The name "fence lizard" was given to

Why do they bob their bodies up and down? these small spiny reptiles because they are often seen clambering over the

stone and wooden fences that mark the boundaries of farms. Like most other small lizards, they will bite when first

Fence lizards, along with spiny and scaly lizards, are known as swifts.

captured. However, the "bite" is more accurately a pinch as they cannot exert enough pressure to drive their small teeth into the skin. Soon after capture they tame down. The males are more brilliantly colored than the females and will sometimes bob their bodies up and down in a fashion that displays these bright colors. These movements are used both to frighten away other males and to attract a mate.

There are about thirty different kinds throughout the United States from the Atlantic to the Pacific, with the exception of the northern tier of states. They feed upon worms, insects and spiders. In captivity, their favorite food is the mealworm.

A five-lined skink of the eastern U. S. laying eggs.

Skinks

Skinks are smooth waxy-looking lizards that usually live close to the ground. They have relatively short legs, long bodies and tails, and some kinds are very snake-like. The smaller species cannot hurt when they bite, but some of the larger kinds can inflict a painful pinch. It takes an alert hunter to catch them, because they quickly disappear either down the burrows they have dug or between the rocks and debris on the woodland floor. They are often found in moist, decaying logs.

They feed mainly upon insects, but larger specimens capture baby mice and birds. In captivity, they are long-lived if provided with plenty of moisture and a good hiding place. After they become tame, they may even take food — including mealworms and beetles — by hand.

Some species are brilliantly colored with stripes and have bright blue tails. The northern prairie skink, found in the north central states, has bright red cheek patches during the breeding season. Fifteen different kinds are found in the United States.

29

Horned Lizards

These curious lizards, sometimes called horned toads, are found in the middle and southwestern United States. Perhaps their flat, squat bodies, short stubby legs, and their sitting posture, caused the early naturalists to call them "horned toads." The presence of body scales immediately identifies them as reptiles. The long hornlike spines on head and body are probably a form of protection. However, hawks, owls, roadrunners, and other lizards are not deterred by these sharp spines when they feed upon the horned lizards.

Why are they called horned toads?

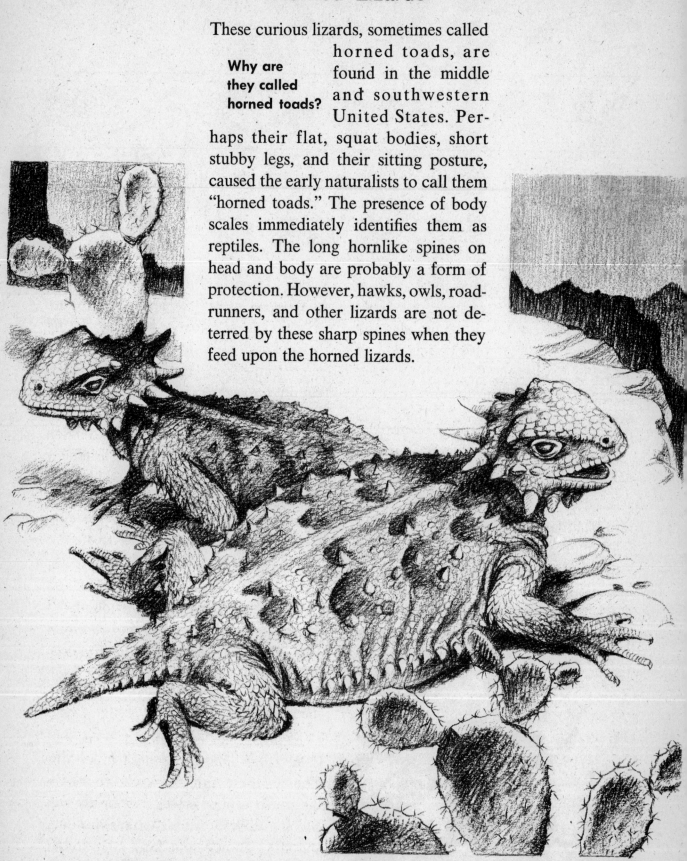

Horned lizards include such species as the short-horned lizard, desert horned lizard and Texas horned lizard.

The word *chameleon* comes from words meaning "ground lion." The American chameleon is also called an anole.

When danger threatens, these lizards will quickly bury them-

How do they protect themselves? selves in loose sand or will puff up their bodies until they are almost twice their normal size. They also have the strange habit of squirting blood from the forward corners of the eyes.

Chameleons are lizards that live in trees

What are chameleons? and prey on insects, as well as on small birds and reptiles. They have a very long, sticky tongue which they keep bundled up in their throat until ready to strike. Their tongue shoots out like a whip and pulls the victim back into the mouth. Chameleons are famous for their complicated color changes; their skin assumes the color patterns of their surroundings. Such camouflage makes them nearly invisible.

The small American "green lizard" is not a true chameleon, but it, too, has the ability to change color.

Under the lizard's skin are a number of tiny cells which are

How do they change their color? branched. They look like tiny trees. These cells contain a pigment (color). When the lizard is excited, frightened, suddenly cooled or heated, or moved into the light or dark, the pigments move to different places in the branches of the cells. If they move toward the surface of the skin, one color is dominant, or stands out. If they move away from the surface, another color is dominant. In this way, the lizard's color can change from dark brown to light green. During courtship and sometimes when the lizard is excited, it will extend a fold of bright red skin at its throat. The toes of this lizard, like those of the geckos, have adhesive-like tips which enable the toes to adhere to smooth surfaces. These small lizards make interesting pets, and readily feed upon mealworms and other small insects.

Snakes

The temperature of warm-blooded animals is always constant, because it is made by the animal's body. The snakes, as well as all other reptiles, are cold-blooded animals.

Where do snakes spend the winter?

The temperature of their bodies is controlled by the temperature of their surroundings. Those kinds that live in the temperate zones, where the winters are severe, find places beneath the ground or in the mud at the bottom of ponds, where the temperature never falls below freezing. Here they spend the winter in a deep "sleep" (hibernation). We do not find reptiles in the cold areas of the Arctic and the Antarctic.

The reptiles that live in tropical countries, where the temperature is often very high, seek hiding places and wait (estivate) for the heat to pass.

Snakes are different from other reptiles in that they have no eyelids or ears. To hear, they sense the vibrations that are carried through the ground, and to protect their eyes they have transparent "caps" through which they see.

How do snakes hear?

When a snake needs to shed its outer layer of skin, it usually picks a quiet, protected spot. There it lies still for a few days while a special oily substance flows between the under layer of skin and the old outer skin, and then hardens. Then the snake moves about to find a rough log or stone upon which it rubs its head to loosen the skin at the edges of its lips. By catching the loose skin on a rough spot, it can crawl out of the old skin in about the same way that we might remove a pair of gloves from our hands — by simply turning them inside out.

How does a snake shed its skin?

This rattlesnake catches its loose skin on a cactus plant in order to shed.

King Snake

King snakes are found in most parts of the United States. Their **What do they eat?** name was probably derived from the fact that they feed upon other snakes, even the poisonous ones. They kill by constriction and are believed to be partially free from the poisonous effects of venomous reptiles. Besides eating other snakes, they feed on rodents, lizards, insects and birds, as well as the eggs of birds. They live in many habitats, but the greater majority seek the woodlands, finding shelter in rotting stumps, under the loose bark of fallen trees, and among rocks and leaves.

They are easily managed in captivity and can be handled **How do king snakes differ from coral snakes?** freely. However, all reptiles have individual temperaments, so some king snakes never tame down. Collecting some of the brilliantly colored king snakes should be done with

KING SNAKE

CORAL SNAKE

great care. Their coloring and pattern are quite similar to those of the very poisonous coral snakes. Coral snakes have a series of bright colored bands along the body and the colors red and yellow come into contact. These two colors never touch in the harmless king snakes.

Hognose Snake

Its upturned snout is a good characteristic for quick identification when we find this short heavy-bodied snake in the field. The snout is

How can you identify it?

used by the snake for digging. It will burrow beneath the surface of sandy soil in quest of toads, which are the main part of its diet. It also eats young mice and lizards.

When molested, this snake displays very unusual behavior. It first flattens its head and spreads the forward part of its body, hisses loudly and strikes out at the danger with a closed mouth. If the annoyance persists, it will soon begin to writhe and twist its body as if in great agony. The hognose snake continues this behavior and finally rolls

How does it "play dead"?

HOGNOSE SNAKE

over on its back, suddenly ceasing all motion. In this condition, it can be prodded without response. However, if we roll it over, right side up, it will immediately roll over onto its back again. Perhaps this snake believes that the only way to act like a dead snake is to lie upside down. They make interesting pets, and once these snakes feel perfectly safe, they will stop "playing dead." It is necessary to have toads available as a food supply for them.

Garter Snakes

Every state in the United States has its populations of garter snakes. These common snakes, which are eighteen to thirty inches in length, are known to every young boy who has spent any time in the field. They can be found in vacant lots, backyards and even city parks. They have a preference for moist places, because there they find their food which consists of worms,

Why do they give off a vile-smelling body fluid?

salamanders, fish and frogs. Young garter snakes will feed readily on insects. When these reptiles are first captured they will give off a vile-smelling fluid from glands at the base of the tail. The odor of this fluid probably repels their enemies. This habit stops as soon as they become tame.

Garter snakes are extremely easy to keep, because they can often be induced to take small pieces of meat and fish as a substitute diet. Care should be taken that large females are put into tight cages. A single female can give birth to as many as fifty or more

How many young can a female garter snake have?

GARTER SNAKE

COPPERHEAD

TIMBER RATTLESNAKE

WESTERN DIAMONDBACK RATTLESNAKE

QUEEN SNAKE

WATER MOCCASIN

RAINBOW SNAKE

CORN SNAKE

Mud snakes cannot roll like hoops, but because of this false belief, they are also called hoop snakes. The stinger (shown in insert, left) is not poisonous.

four-to-five-inch young. The name of this snake undoubtedly comes from its ribbon-like pattern, which is similar to that on the ribbon garters used by men.

Mud Snake

These long blue-black snakes are found in the southeastern part of the United States, and are four to six feet long. They are docile and can easily be tamed. They live along the fresh-water canals and swamps where they catch fish and large salamanders for food. The bright red patches of color on the sides and underparts of the body are in strong contrast to the black ground color.

However, the snake is not easily discovered, because it usually **Can it** hides in the muddy water **roll like** when molested. The tail ter- **a hoop?** minates in a sharp spine-like tip. When handled, this harmless tip will often scratch across the skin. This has caused many false stories to be told about the mud snake, such as: "It stings you with the end of its 'poisonous' tail"; "It can take its tail into its mouth and roll like a hoop." Both stories are not true, of course.

In captivity, these snakes should be provided with plenty of water. An aquarium tank, partially filled, makes an adequate cage. A large rock should be provided so that the snake can get up out of the water when necessary.

Small Snakes

Where can you find small snakes?

Twelve inches and under is the adult size of many snakes that live in the United States. The smaller varieties are as interesting and striking in appearance as many of the larger forms, and often they can be found close to human habitation. We can discover these reptiles by carefully turning over rocks, leaves and rotting wood that lie on the ground in a vacant lot, field or remote corner of the city park.

In the eastern and central United States we can find worm snakes, red-bellied snakes, De Kay snakes, ring-neck snakes, Florida brown snakes, rough and smooth earth snakes, and black swamp snakes. Many of these snakes are quite colorful. The red-bellied snake and the black swamp snake possess bright red ventral (underpart) scales. De Kay snakes have a soft brown dorsal (upper) surface. When the animal is disturbed and puffs up its body, the dorsal surface turns into a checkerboard pattern. The ring-neck snake has a striking color and pattern. The undersides are either a bright red or orange red, the back is a glossy blue-gray, and about the neck there is a collar of bright yellow. There are also many small species in the western part of the United States.

All small snakes feed upon insects, worms, small salamanders and fish, and they can be easily tamed and kept for study in your own home "zoo."

Pictured above is a den of rattlers. Rattlesnakes are born alive and a litter of about one dozen is common.

How to Keep Reptiles

The most important thing in caring for wild animals is cleanliness. The cages have to be kept spotlessly clean and each animal needs plenty of fresh drinking water. Aquatic turtles and alligators can be kept in aquarium tanks which hold about one or two inches of water. A couple of large flat stones are needed, so that the animals can climb up out of the water. Clean these tanks at least twice a week and always be sure that the new water is the same temperature as that which was removed.

Feed the reptiles once a week by putting small pieces of raw fish or meat directly onto the stones. Any of the food not eaten has to be removed before the end of the day. Both alligators and turtles grasp the food and carry it off into the water before swallowing it.

Cages in which sand, earth, small cactus plants and other natural decorations are placed do look natural. However, it is difficult to keep this type of cage clean and it is not long before disease establishes itself. The best place to keep lizards, snakes and land turtles is in a small, simple, well-ventilated cage which is painted with a hard, glossy enamel paint. Such cages are easy to keep clean and dry.

The only foreign object that should be put into a reptile cage, besides a drinking dish, is something that will give the reptile a place to hide. An inverted cardboard shoe box, with a small hole cut in the side, makes a good reptile home.

The joy of learning about the living things around us can come from keeping a wild animal as a pet.

Reptiles make good pets.

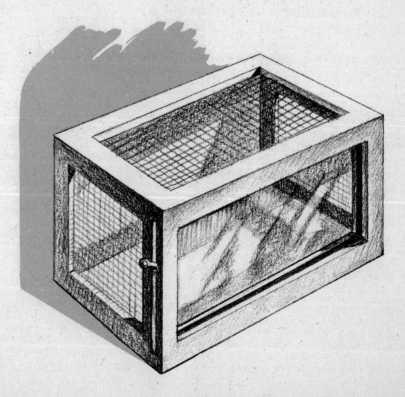

A simple, well-ventilated cage is the best home for your reptile.

CAGE FOR SNAKES

CAGE FOR SEMI-AQUATIC SPECIMENS

CAGE FOR LIZARDS

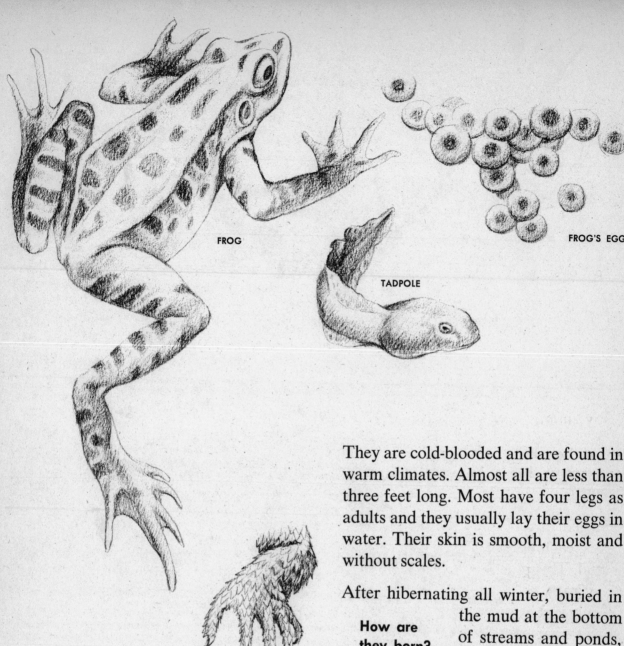

FROG

FROG'S EGGS

TADPOLE

FOOT OF LIZARD

Amphibians

Amphibians are a class of backboned

What are amphibians? animals which are specially adapted for life in the water when they are young, and on the land when they are adults. They include frogs, toads, salamanders, and caecilians, which look like worms. To characterize amphibians generally, their young breathe by means of gills and as adults, usually have lungs.

They are cold-blooded and are found in warm climates. Almost all are less than three feet long. Most have four legs as adults and they usually lay their eggs in water. Their skin is smooth, moist and without scales.

After hibernating all winter, buried in

How are they born? the mud at the bottom of streams and ponds, frogs and toads emerge in the spring to renew their life cycle. The females lay eggs in a jelly-like mass, attaching them to twigs, grass, or stones in shallow water. In a short time — from a few days to a few weeks, depending on the kind of amphibian and the temperature of the water — the eggs hatch into tadpoles or larvae. These tiny creatures are completely on their own and soon learn to nibble at small water plants and hide from their enemies. Eventually, the tadpole's gills disappear, its tail shrinks, and it begins to grow legs.

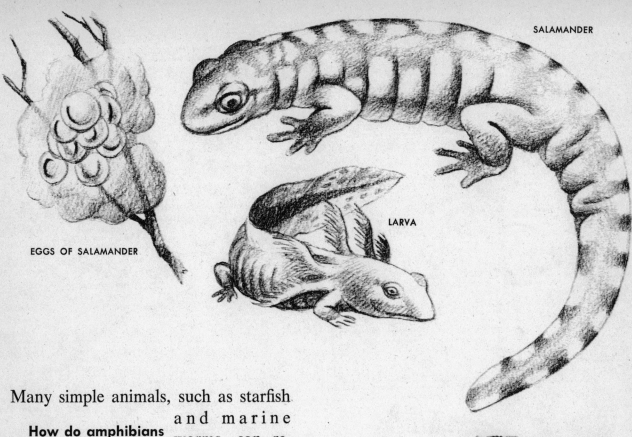

EGGS OF SALAMANDER

LARVA

SALAMANDER

SKIN OF FROG

SKIN OF LIZARD

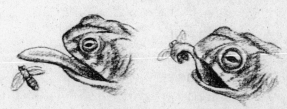

HOW TOAD CATCHES PREY

Many simple animals, such as starfish and marine worms, can rebuild themselves if their body is damaged. If a starfish is cut into large pieces, each piece will grow into a new animal. This process is called *regeneration*. Frogs, toads, and salamanders are the only vertebrates (animals with backbones) that can regenerate legs and tails.

How do amphibians regenerate body parts?

In 1768, the Italian naturalist Lazzaro Spallanzani discovered that tadpoles can regrow a missing limb, but that they lose this ability upon becoming a full-grown frog. He also observed that when a salamander's leg is cut off, a new limb grows from the stump within several weeks. The regenerated limb is perfect in every way, complete with muscles, bones, nerves, and blood vessels. Many scientists have studied regeneration in modern times, but they do not yet understand this mysterious process.

GREEN FROG

BULLFROG

BARKING FROG

GREEN TREE FROG

CRICKET FROG

RED-LEGGED FROG

NARROW-MOUTHED TOAD

AMERICAN TOAD

GREAT PLAINS TOAD

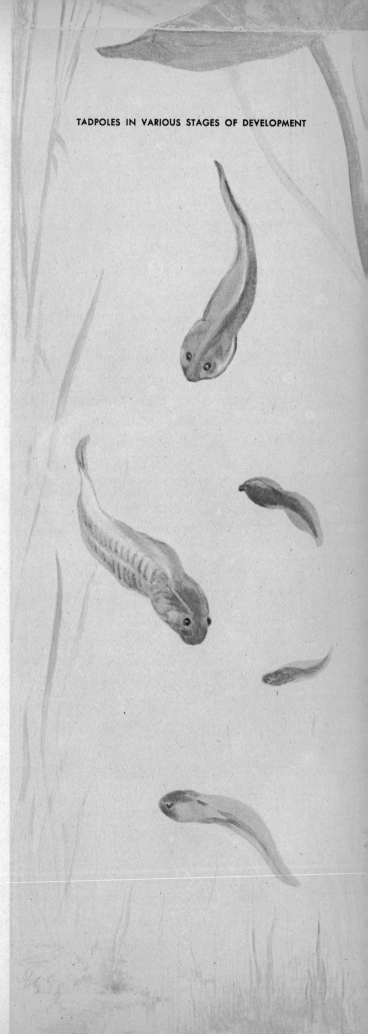

TADPOLES IN VARIOUS STAGES OF DEVELOPMENT

Wood Frog

What does it look like? Like many wild creatures, frogs are endowed with protective colors which blend with their natural habitat. For example, the wood frog is soft brown like the leaves and leaf mold in the woods where it lives. Looking closely at the wood frog, we can see other interesting characteristics. Its hind legs, long and strong, allow it to jump many times its own length, and the wood frog turns in mid-air to face its enemy when it lands. Its bulging eyes are bright-colored, like jewels, but it sees moving objects better than still ones. Its wide mouth allows it to gulp down its food whole — smaller frogs, worms, snails and small fish. Its long, sticky tongue flips out like lightning to capture insects in flight.

Wood frogs lay a mass of 2,000 to 3,000 eggs.

Tree Frogs

Can frogs climb trees? We usually think of frogs jumping on the ground, but tree frogs actually live in trees and shrubs, where they cling to branches with the help of sticky pads on their toes. These little frogs, no more than two inches in length, leave their airy homes only to lay their eggs at breeding time. There are several species in addition to the common tree frog, which has a dark patch on its back. The green tree frog is bright green and can change its color quickly. The Canyon tree frog has several round spots on its back, and the Pacific tree frog is striped.

How do frogs catch their food? Everyone who has observed frogs in their natural setting knows that a frog's jump is very fast and very accurate — precise enough to catch a fly several feet away. High-speed photography has revealed that a frog begins its leap by pushing off with its legs, which unfold behind it as it launches itself into the air. While in the air, the frog adjusts its flight path by twisting its hind legs like a high diver. When the frog is within three inches of its prey, it turns its mouth under its victim, drops its lower jaw, and flips out its tongue. The tongue wraps itself around its victim like a whip and pulls it back into its mouth. The entire jump takes about three-tenths of a second, and the food is snatched and gobbled up in a mere one-tenth of a second.

Spadefoot Toad

Do toads cause warts? It is difficult to distinguish between toads and frogs until we remember that toads have a rough or warty skin, that they are more plump and move more slowly than frogs, and that they do not always live near water. It is not true, of course, that toads will cause warts if you handle them, but when they are in danger their skin sometimes exudes a milky fluid. Most toads burrow into the ground, and the spadefoot toad is especially well

The spadefoot leaves its burrow at night to feed.

equipped for burrowing. It has webbed, spadelike feet which clear the way as it twists itself backward into the soil.

Newts

What is the newt's life cycle? Of all the salamanders — and there are more than a hundred different kinds in the United States — the newt has the most interesting life cycle. Its eggs, similar to those of the frog, are deposited on leaves and stems of water plants. After hatching, the larvae live for three or four months in the water and then come out onto dry land. It is now bright orange in color with red spots circled in black on its back. After spending two or three years on land and growing to three or four inches in length, it returns to water for the rest of its life. The adults of the eastern newts then change color and develop a broad swimming tail which helps them move about.

Blind Salamanders

Why is it called "blind"? A great variety of salamanders is to be found in various parts of the United States. Among the aquatic species are the mud puppy, hellbender and Congo eel. Some salamanders have names descriptive of their color or markings: green, purple, red, painted, tiger, mottled and marbled.

Salamanders are not as commonly seen as frogs and toads, because many of them come out only at night and all of them avoid the sun. One species, the blind salamander, usually lives in caves, and its eyes are either very small or undeveloped. Because it lives in darkness, its skin is pale yellow or white. These salamanders are found in the Ozarks, Georgia and Texas.

MUD PUPPY

SLIMY SALAMANDER

RED SALAMANDER

ALLIGATOR SALAMANDER

YELLOW SPOTTED SALAMANDER

PAINTED SALAMANDER

DEVELOPMENT OF NEWT